The Wildbore Family of Kent England

by Lorine McGinnis Schulze

ISBN: 978-1-987938-12-8
Copyright 2017
All rights reserved
Publisher Olive Tree Genealogy

Over the last 40 plus years I have researched and gathered a great deal of information and uncovered many documents for my mother's ancestors in England. Pondering how best to preserve my research and share the stories of these maternal ancestors, I decided to compile books on each family surname.

Because the books were written for family, I have not cited my sources nor have I written long chapters of anecdotal stories. Instead I opted to create a chronological timeline for each generation. Images for all baptismal, marriage, burial, land records and so on that were discovered for each ancestor are also included.

If siblings were found, family group sheets are included. If they were not found, only my direct ancestor is noted. At the end of the book you will find blank pages for your own notes.

Those who want to know my sources can contact me directly through my website Olive Tree Genealogy at www.OliveTreeGenealogy.com My email is found at the bottom of each page.

I hope that readers enjoy these books and the stories of the ancestors.

Lorine McGinnis Schulze

Table of Contents

Wildbore Family of Kent England 1

11th Great-Grandfather George Wildbore aka Wildboar 1550-1606 3

10th Great-Grandfather Edward Wildbore aka Wildboar 1580-1642 10

9th Great-Grandfather Nicholas Wildbore aka Wildboar 1611-? 12

8th Great-Grandfather Thomas Wildbore aka Wildboar 14

7th Great-Grandmother Ann Wildbore 20

Notes 21

Wildbore Family of Kent England

The Wildbore family is found in Minster, Thanet, Kent England as far back as 1550. The surname has been found as Wildbore, Wildebore, Wildboar and Wilbore. The earliest church records for St. Mary, Minster do not exist before 1557 and thus this 1550 baptism of my 11th great-grandfather George Wildbore is not found. The first official document is his marriage to Alice (Alicia) Pamphlet in 1571 recorded in St. Mary Minster.

St. Mary the Virgin church in Minster, Thanet, Kent England

By John Salmon, CC BY-SA 2.0,
https://commons.wikimedia.org/w/index.php?curid=5115381

 Georgius Wildbore. It has a certain strength when you say it out loud. I imagine the man who had this name bestowed on him - strong, tall, a brave warrior...... but in all likelihood he was short, thin and stoop-shouldered from years of toil.

Georgius was my 11th Great-grandfather on my maternal side, and he was born ca 1550 in Kent England, probably in Thanet. I suspect he was a farmer, struggling to grow a few crops in the tiny parish town of St. Mary Minster, for that is where he married, raised his 7 known children, and died in 1606.

I am lucky to have found a copy of Georgius' will but it is not easy reading. In the will he is named as George Wildbore which is a bit of a letdown from the romantic notion of a strong and regal Gregorius. But reality is reality and I know that Georgius was just the Latin rendition of his very ordinary name.

In his will, which I have struggled with for many years, I have only been able so far to read "Alice my wife and Edward Wildbore my son" (Edward, who was baptised in 1580, is my 10th great-grandfather) and "Joan [Colly?] the wife of Thomas [Colly?]" and "Jeremie Wildbore my son".

It is fascinating to me to learn that Minster in Thanet originally started as a monastic settlement in 670AD. The parish church of St. Mary-the-Virgin was built during Norman times. It is quite possible that my ancestors go back to this time. I have literally dozens of surnames of ancestors who lived and died in this small area from at least the early 1500s to mid 1800s.

11th Great-Grandfather George Wildbore aka Wildboar 1550-1606

Georgorius (George) Wildbore was born circa 1550 in Kent England. His marriage is recorded on 09 Jul 1571 in St. Mary Minster, Thanet, Kent. His bride was Alicia (Alice) Pamphlet. Although it is not noted in the surviving church record, we know that Alice was a widow, having married Gilbert Pamphlet (Pamflet) in Thanet in 1563. Her maiden name was Sackett and she was the sister of Richard Sackett as stated in his will.

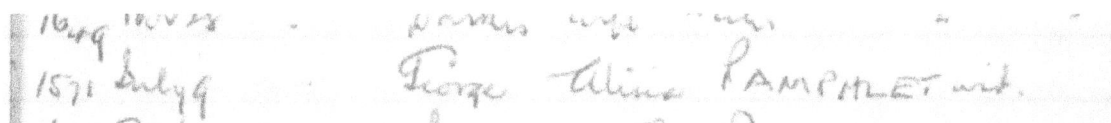

WILDBORE extractions found in the Tyler Index to Parish Registers for Minster in Thanet, Kent

Here we see that at the 1571 marriage of George Wildbore and Alice, she is listed as Alicia Pamphlet, wid. (widow)

Alice was named as a beneficiary in her brother Richard's will made in Minster in Thanet on 31 May 1604. She was to receive the tenement and lands at Totthill, Minster, which she and her husband George Wildbore were presently occupying, with reversion to her sons Jeremy and Edward Wildbore.

It may be of interest to note details about Richard Sackett. Richard made his will in Minster in Thanet on 31 May 1604. He left a tenement and lands at Totthill, Minster to his sister Alice, with reversion to her sons Jeremy and Edward. He left £20 to Agnes Wildbore and £10 to Barbara Wildbore, daughter of Jeremy.

Richard left his home tenement and lands at Minster to Denise, wife of John Peele, with reversion to Denise's sons William and John Peele. He left lands at Brooke, Minster, to Mary, wife of John Hancock. Richard's will was proved at Canterbury on 12 December 1604.

Thanks to the Sackett Family Association we have the following extract:

Will of Richard Sackett of Minster in Thanet, Kent, 31 May 1604, proved in the Canterbury Archdeaconry Court, 12 December 1604 (Kent Archives Office, PRC 17-54-305). (Researched by Michael Callé).

Richard Sackett, yeoman of Minster in Thanet, 31 May 1604, proved in the Archdeaconry Court of Canterbury 12 December 1604.

Beneficiaries
Sister Alice Wilbore - tenement & lands at Totthill, Minster, occupied by John Bright

& George Wilbore
Jeremy & Edward Wilbore, sons of Alice - reversion of above
Denise Peele, wife of John - tenement & lands at Minster in own occupation, & lands in occupation of Richard Terrie of Chislett & Edward Allen of Minster
William & John Peele, sons of Denise - reversion of above
Mary J/Hancock, wife of John - lands at Brooke, Minster
George & William Tomlyn, sons of John - [legacy omitted from register]
Agnes Wilbore - £20
Barbara Wilbore, dau of Jeremy - £10
Joane Solly, wife of Thomas - 40/-
Denise Derrick, wife of Robert of Birchington - 40/-
Daniel Pamphlet - residue

Executor - Daniel Pamphlet

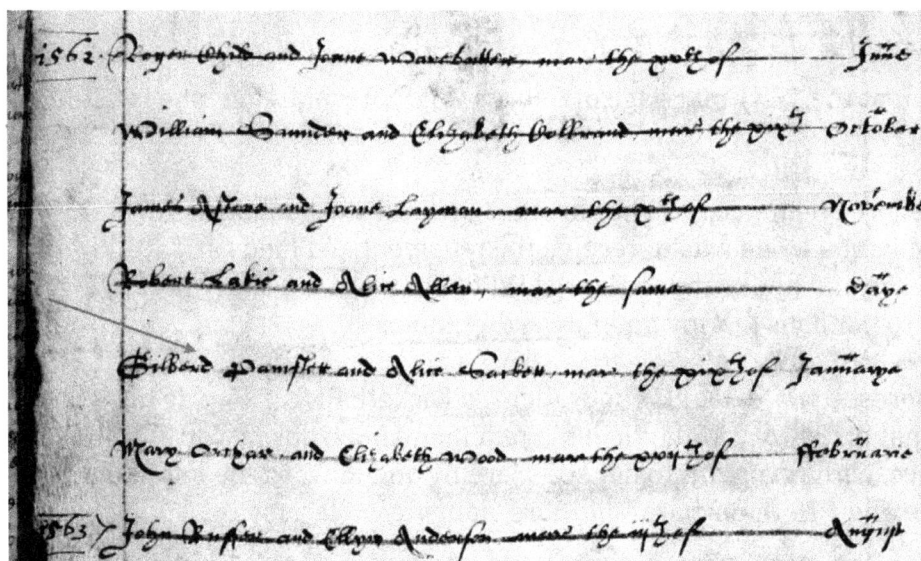

1563 marriage of Alice Sackett and Gilbert Pamflet

George Wildbore and Alice had 7 known children: Thomasin, Nicholas, Jeremy, Edward (my 10th great-grandfather), Anna, and twins Susanna & John.

On 26 Feb 1606/07 George died. Alice died 10 years later on 03 Aug 1616.

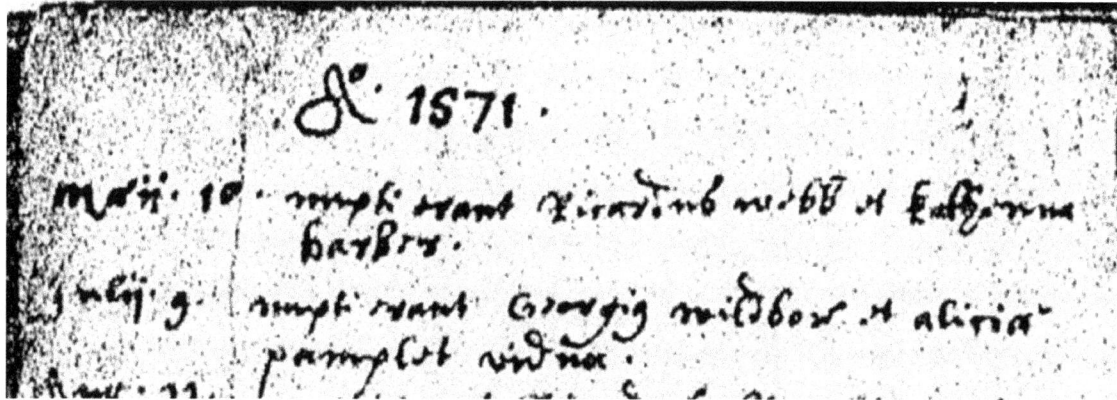

Marriage of George (Gregorius) Wildbore and Alice Pamphlet, widower.   9 July1571

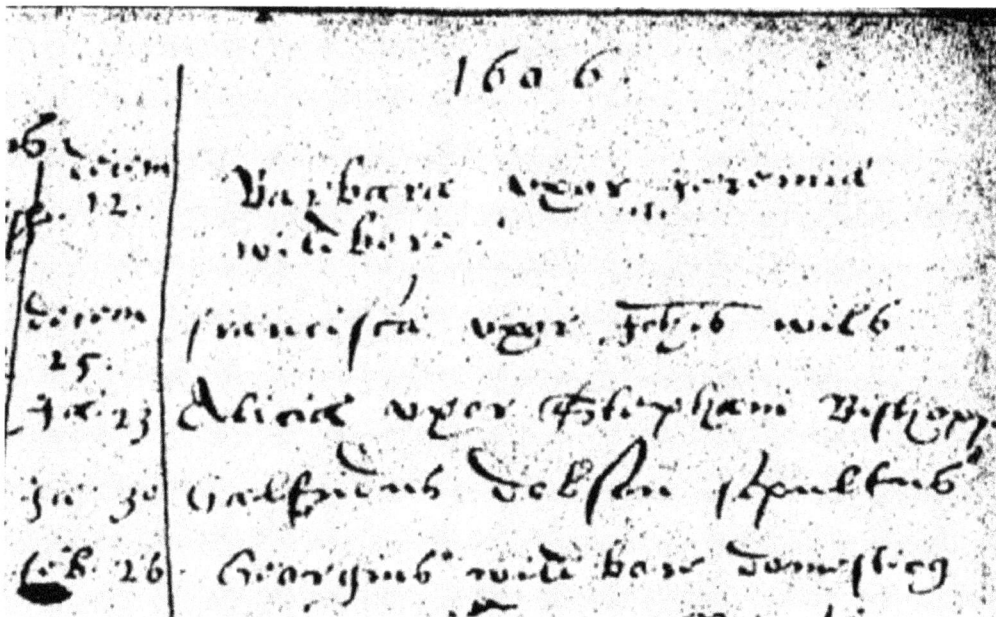

Death Record of George (Gregorius) Wildbore in 1606

Feb. 1606 Will of George Wildbore of Minster, Thanet Kent

The burial of Alicia Wildbore took place on 3 August 1616 from St. Mary the Virgin in Minster, Thanet England.

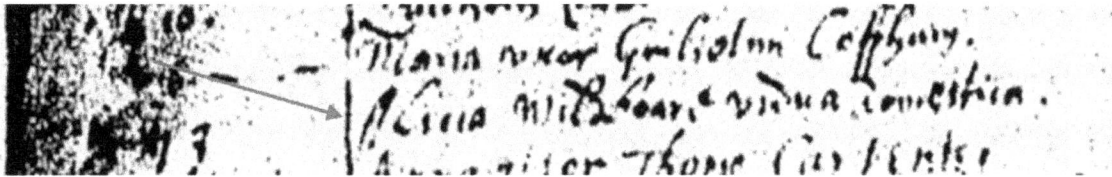

Family Group Sheet for Georgorius (George) Wildbore

Husband:		Georgorius (George) Wildbore
	b:	Abt. 1550
	m:	09 Jul 1571 in St. Mary Minster, Thanet, Kent, Eng.
	d:	26 Feb 1606/07 in St. Mary Minster, Thanet, Kent, Eng.
	Father:	
	Mother:	
Wife:		Alicia (Alice) Sackett
	b:	Abt. 1548 in Thanet, Kent England
	d:	03 Aug 1616 in St. Mary Minster, Thanet, Kent, Eng.
	Father:	
	Mother:	
Children:		
1	Name:	Tomasine Wildbore
F	b:	29 Jul 1572
	d:	01 Jul 1585 in Minster in Thanet, Kent England
2	Name:	Nicolas Wildbore
M	b:	08 Jun 1575
3	Name:	Jeremy Wildbore
M	b:	14 May 1578
	m:	19 Oct 1601 in Minster in Thanet, Kent England
	d:	26 Jun 1616 in Minster in Thanet, Kent England
	Spouse:	Barbara Mercer
4	Name:	Edward Wildbore
M	b:	13 Dec 1580 in St.. Mary Minster, Thanet, Kent, Eng.
	m:	08 Oct 1610 in Canterbury, Eng.
	d:	16 Mar 1642 in Minster in Thanet, St Mary the Virgin, Kent Enland
	Spouse:	Mary Webb
5	Name:	Anna Wildbore
F	b:	25 May 1584
6	Name:	Susanna Wildbore
F	b:	11 Jun 1588
7	Name:	John Wildbore
M	b:	11 Jun 1588

Edward Wildbore is my next direct ancestor and is discussed in the next chapter but since Jeremy Wildbore is mentioned in his uncle's will I am including information I found on his family group.

Jeremy is also found in the records as Jeremiah. In October 1601 he married the widow Barbara Cropper in Minster in Thanet.

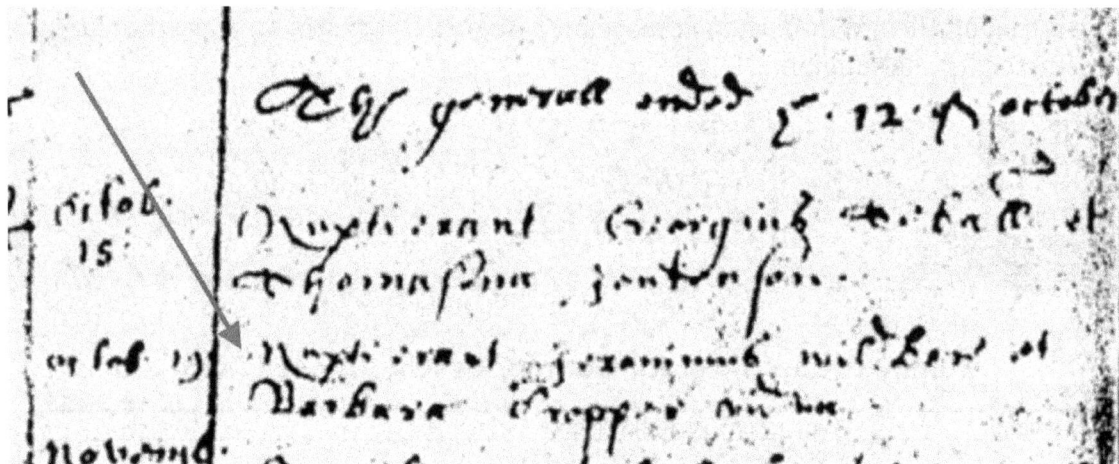

Marriage in 1601 of Jeremiah Wildbore and Barbara Cropper, widow.

Barbara's previous marriage to Ralph (also known as Radolphus) Cropper aka Cropp, took place in Minster on 30 May 1588. Her maiden name was given as Mercer.

Ralph and Barbara had 3 known children – Ursula born in 1594, William born in 1597, and Bartholomew born in 1599. Little Bartholomew only lived 4 months then died in March 1600 just 3 weeks before his father Ralph died.

Church records indicate that Barbara and Jeremy had two children before her death in 1606.

1 August 1602 Barbara d. Jeremie Wildbore.
13 Januar 1604/05 George s. Jeremie Wildbore.

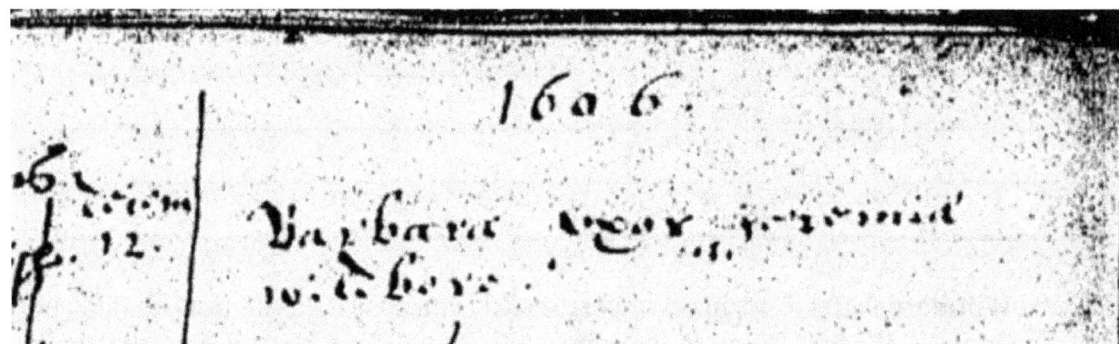

Burial record of Barbara, wife of Jeremiah Wildbore December 12, 1606

Jeremy had more children so at some point after Barbara's death in 1606 and the birth of his daughter Susanna in 1610, he remarried. I have not found his second marriage record. But the church records provide details on three more children born to him before he too died in 1616. At the baptism of his son Jeremie in September 1616, he was noted as deceased. His burial is recorded as June 26 the same year, two months before his son was born.

16 September 1610 Susanna d. Jeremie Wildbore."
9 May 1613 Thos s. Jeremie Wildbore.
1 Sep 1616 Jeremie s. Jeremie Wildbore.

10th Great-Grandfather Edward Wildbore aka Wildboar 1580-1642

Edward was baptised in St. Mary on 13 Dec 1580. On 08 October 1610 he married Mary Webb in Canterbury. Mary was noted in the register as being a virgin. There was a separate designation for a spinster so one wonders how Mary proved her virginity!

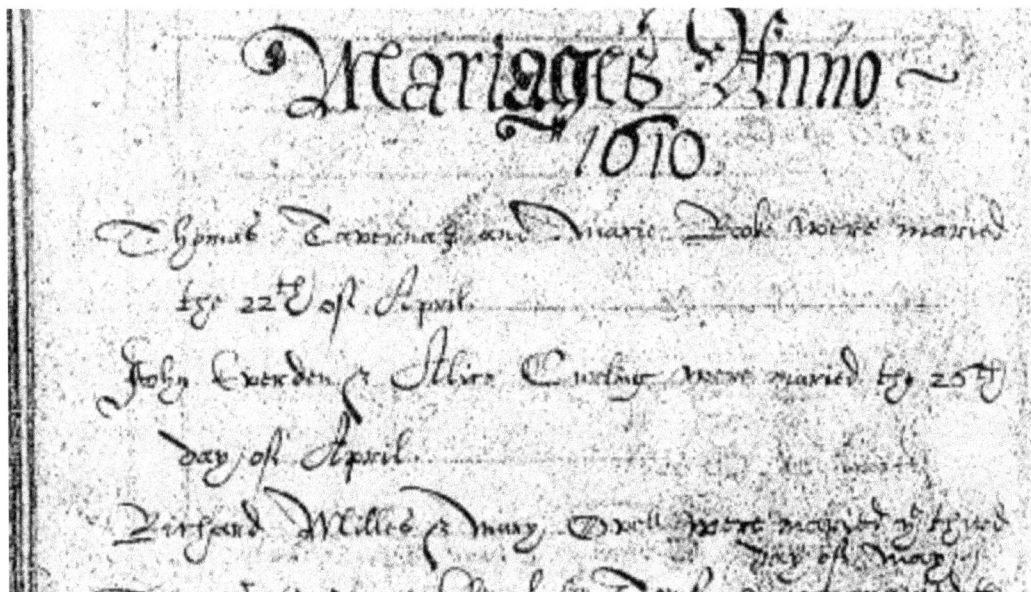

Marriage of Edward Wildbore & Mary Webb in 1610

Wildebore, Edward, of Minster in Thanet, husb., and Mary Webb, s. p., v. At St. George's, Cant. Oct. 8, 1610.

husb.=husbandman   s.p.=of the same parish/of the same place   v. =virgin

Little is known of Mary Webb's origins except what is noted in the marriage record – that both she and Edward were living in Minster in Thanet.

The couple had 5 known children: Nicholas (our ancestor), John, Isaac, Elizabeth & Mary. On 16 March 1642 Edward died and was buried at St. Mary the Virgin in Minster.

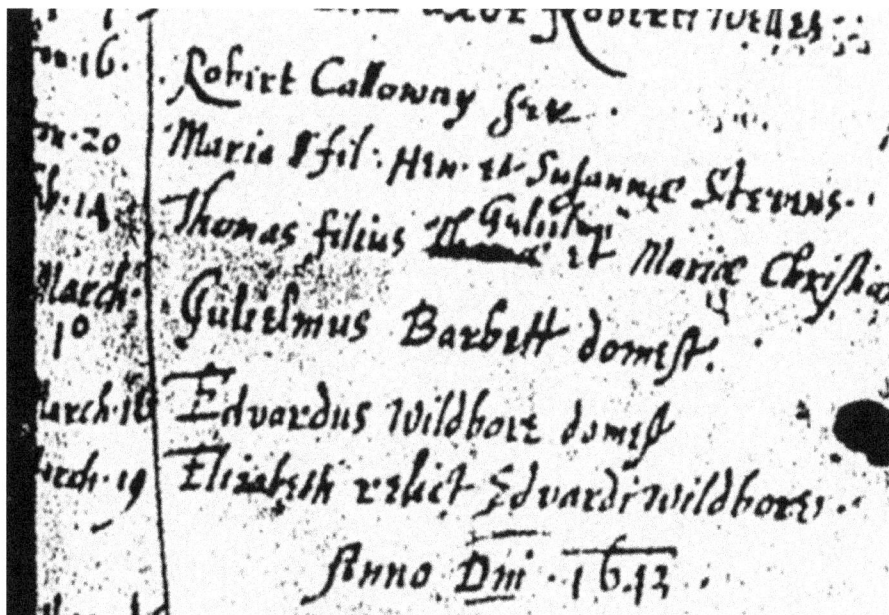

Burial of Edward (Edwardus) Wildbore in 1642

Family Group Sheet for Edward Wildbore

Husband:		Edward Wildbore
	b:	13 Dec 1580 in St.. Mary Minster, Thanet, Kent, Eng.
	m:	08 Oct 1610 in Canterbury, Eng.
	d:	16 Mar 1642 in Minster in Thanet, St Mary the Virgin, Kent Enland
	Father:	Georgorius (George) Wildbore
	Mother:	Alicia (Alice) Sackett
Wife:		Mary Webb
	b:	Bet. 1580-1590
	Father:	
	Mother:	
Children:		
1	Name:	Nicolas Wildbore
M	b:	10 Nov 1611 in St. Mary Minster, Thanet, Kent, Eng.
	m:	20 Oct 1636 in Thanet, Kent Eng
	Spouse:	Dorcas Norwood
2	Name:	John Wildbore
M	b:	03 Apr 1614
3	Name:	Isaac Wildbore
M	b:	25 Mar 1620
	m:	06 Aug 1643 in Minster in Thanet, Kent England
	Spouse:	Anne Paine
4	Name:	Elizabeth Wildbore
F	b:	20 Feb 1623/24
5	Name:	Mary Wildbore
F	b:	11 Mar 1625/26

9th Great-Grandfather Nicholas Wildbore aka Wildboar 1611-?

Nicholas was baptised 10 November 1611 in St. Mary the Virgin. On 20 October 1636 he married Dorcas Norwood, the daughter of Stephen and Elizabeth Norwood.

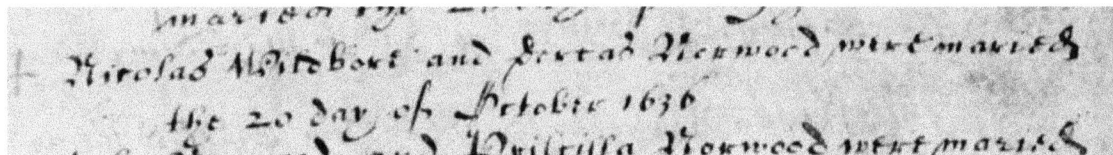

1626 Marriage Nicholas Wildbore & Dorcas Norwood

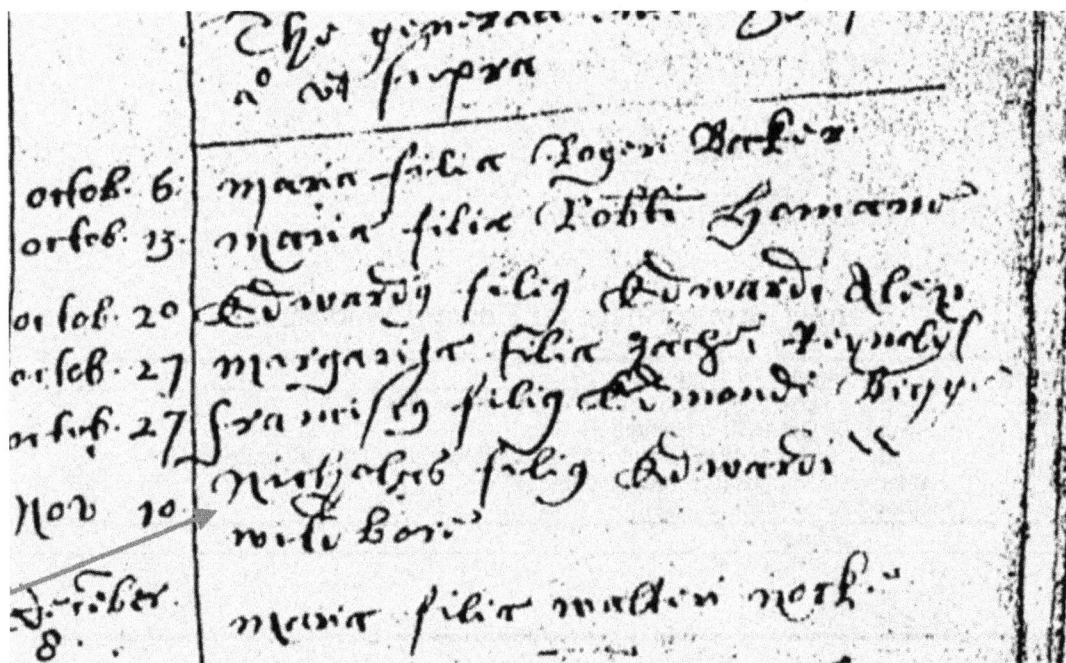

Baptism of Nicholas Wildbore 1611

Nicholas and Dorcas had 6 known children including our next ancestor, Thomas Wildbore.

Family Group Sheet for Nicolas Wildbore

Husband:		Nicolas Wildbore
	b:	10 Nov 1611 in St. Mary Minster, Thanet, Kent, Eng.
	m:	20 Oct 1636 in Thanet, Kent Eng
	Father:	Edward Wildbore
	Mother:	Mary Webb
Wife:		Dorcas Norwood
	b:	10 Jul 1614 in Ash, St Nicholas, Kent England
	d:	28 Nov 1649 in St. Mary Minster, Thanet, Kent, Eng.
	Father:	Stephen Norwood
	Mother:	Elizabeth
Children:		
1	Name:	Edward Wildbore
M	b:	15 Oct 1637 in St. Peter in Thanet, Kent
2	Name:	John Wildbore
M	b:	08 Sep 1639
3	Name:	Edward Wildbore
M	b:	04 Jul 1641
4	Name:	Priscilla Wildbore
F	b:	07 Jul 1644
5	Name:	Dorcas Wildbore
F	b:	24 Aug 1645
6	Name:	Thomas Wildbore
M	b:	Abt. 1648
	m:	07 Apr 1672 in Thanet, Kent England
	Spouse:	Mary Browning

8th Great-Grandfather Thomas Wildbore aka Wildboar

Thomas was born circa 1648 and on 07 Apr 1672 he married Mary Browning in Thanet. She was baptised on 18 Oct 1646, the daughter of John Browning and Anne Norwood. Ann was baptised March 1613 in St. Peter Thanet as daughter of Nicholas Norwood.

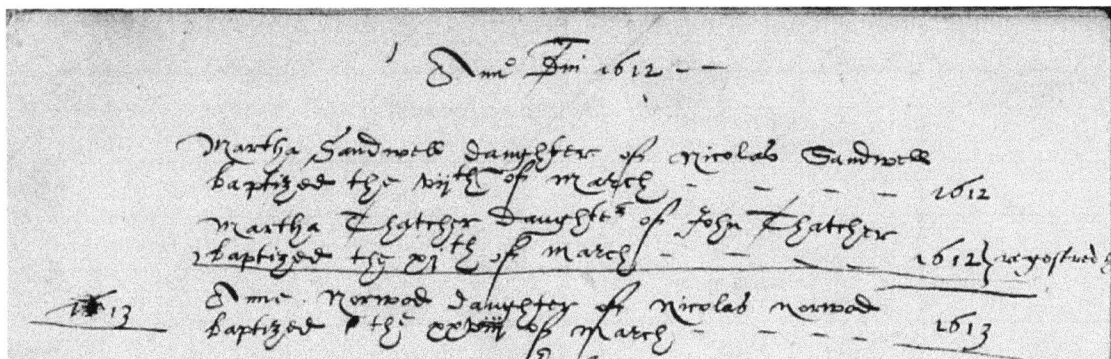

1613 Baptism Anne Norwood (bottom entry)

Nicholas Norwood's name appears on a Muster Roll dated 1 April 1619. He is listed under Corslett. Research seems to indicate that Pikemen wore full Corsletts or leather "armour" of sorts. The other group listed is under Musquetts which is Musketts.

In 1557 a law was passed. Anyone with an income of £1000 a year or more was expected to provide six horses for men-at-arms carrying the shorter lances used in battle (demi-lance), ten geldings equipped with armour and weapons (light-horse), 40 **corslets (suits of armour),** 40 almain rivets (studded jackets), 40 pikes, 30 longbows each with a sheaf of arrows (24), 30 skulls or steep caps, 20 bill or halberd, 20 hackbuts (simple firearms), and 20 morions or sallets (helmets).

About half the men carried hand weapons such as pikes and halberds (including those listed simply as 'armed men') and half carried fire arms such as calivers and muskets; the lower orders made up the 'pioneers', equipped with picks and shovels. The three wagoners were responsible for transport and the two drummers were there to ensure that the soldiers kept pace when marching. Calivers and muskets were precursors to the rifle. The caliver had a barrel between 39 and 44 inches in length, giving the weapon an overall length of about 55 inches; it weighed between 10 and 12 pounds. The musket was much larger and heavier than the caliver, with a barrel between 45 and 55 inches long, and a weight of about 20 pounds; its weight was such that it had to be supported by a forked rest during aiming. **The pikemen, who were expected to be 'the strongest men and best persons' had to fight at close quarters and so had body protection in the form of a corslet, a metal shell around the body, with pouldrons, vambraces and tassets which were metal plates to protect the shoulders, arms and thighs, and gauntlets. To protect their heads the pikemen wore a steel cap or morion well stuffed for**

comfort, tied with a scarf under the chin. The halberd was a shorter weapon, some 7 to 8 feet long, with a metal point like the pike for thrusting, a heavy blade for cutting and a hook for dragging horsemen from their saddles.

The muster role for 1572 for St John's, St Peter's and Birchington combined shows 170 men in the select band and 204 in the general band, giving 374 in total, a total figure very similar to that for 1599. The Muster Role for 1619 shows that the Select Company then contained 147 men, including 3 officers and 2 sergeants, and the General Company contained 172 men including 3 officers and 2 sergeants.[42,47] In the Select Company 60 were Corsletts, pike men named after their corslets or body armour, and 80 were Musquets, with a clerk and a drummer and two waggons looked after by two wagoners. In the General Company 30 were Corsletts, 76 were Musketts, and 60 were 'Dry Pykes' who, it seems, were pike men who wore no armour;[48] there was also one drummer. The officers of the Select Company were listed as 'Paul Cleybrooke, captaine, esquire, Manasses Norwood, Lietenant, gen., and William Cleybrooke, ensigne, gen.' and those of the General Company were listed as 'Valentine Pettit, gent., captayne, William Parker, Liuetenauntt, and Thomas Busher, Ensigne.' Paule Cleybrooke was from Fordwich, Manasses Norwood from Dane Court, William Cleybrooke from Nash Court, Valentine Pettit from Dent de Lyon, and William Parker from Minster, illustrating once again the importance of the large farming families in the Isle of Thanet.

1620 English Pikeman's Armour

The Muster Roule* of the Select Compani in the parishes of S^t
Johns St Peeters and Burchington in thyle of Thanett in the
County of Kent containeing the names of the Captain
officers and souldyers of the same.

Paule Cleybrooke, captaine, esquire
Manasses Norwood, Liuetenant, gen.
William Cleybrooke, ensigne, gen.
Richard Gosby }
Thomas Crafte } Sargants
Henry Jones clerke
Nathaniell Waighyll Drummer

Corslotts.

John Cocklinge	Richard Hallett	Nicholas Norwood
Pecter Swynford	Henry Stedman	Edward Adderfull
John Sharpe	Henry Pett	John Smyth
John Hodges	John Pynck	William Symons
Samuell Legate	Robert Edinger	Henry Penny
George Pett	John Wyther	Adam Coosin
John Tomlyn	William Tomlyn	Thomas Boyes
Elias Arnold	Richard Reynolds	John Adye
Thomas Poole	Thomas Nashe	Thomas Kempe
Robert Gore	John Sackett	William Reynoldes
John Pannell	Robert Gusson	James Nicholas
Alexander ffleete	Edward Wyle sen.	Henry Careys
Nicholas Owenden	Henry Graunt	William Colman
George Totenham	James Boykett	John Smyth
Thomas Kennytt	William Graunt	John Austen
Robert ffurman	Robert Norwood jun^r	John Johnson
Robert Vincle	Edward ffuller	Richard Maye
John Greenstreete	Thomas Emtage	Daniell ffreind. 60.
Nicholas Woolman	Thomas Smyth	
Edward Wytherden	George Marley	

Musquets.

Gylbert Dod	Abdias Peerce	Heugh Johnson
William Payne	Thomas ffuller	Zachary Byllinghurst
Thomas Wheatly	James Jones	John Martin
Henry Pannell	Daniell Pamphett	John Laminge

390   THANET.

Musquets.

William Laminge   John Smyth   John Sprackling
Anthony Curlinge   Mathew Jinkinson   John Phylpott
Paule Graunt   Robert Yonge   Edward Start
Zachary Ranshorne   William ffantinge   Robert Graunt
John Elsetter   John Hewes   Nicholas Dawson
Richard Polin   Rowland Shurth   Thomas Norwood
John Pantry   William Sackett jun'   Lewis Maxsted
George Abbott   James Stone   Michaell Norwood
William Spryngett   Andrew Langly   George Wytherden
William Sackett sen'   John Thurlo   James Weste
Richard Muzred   Edward Jinkyn   Richard Gee
John Goodwyn   William Samson   William Vffington
Edward Toddy   Roger Laminge   John Ayers
William Hinchawe   Thomas Elwood   John ffoxe
Austen Lushenden   Jeremy Samson   Richard Mockett
Symon Owery   George Baldocke   Edward Colman
Thomas Brooman   John Cullmer   Vincent Underdowne
Michaell Greedier   Robert Reade   Mathewe Cantis
John Prince   John Stone   William Norwood
Robert Wythers   Michaell Polin   Thomas Cullmer
John Gosby   William Chiles   William Jordan
Robert Peerce   Thomas ffleete   Richard Colman
William Alexander   Gylford Cullmer   Robert Cavell
Henry Collmer   Valentine Cocklinge   Robert Cwimiell ? 80

                         Waggons two.

                Waggoners { Robert Reade.
                          { Robert Edinger.

(Signed)   PAULE CLEAYBROOKE, Capt.
                Apryll the first 1619.

7th Great-Grandmother Ann Wildbore

Thomas and Ann's daughter Ann Wildbore was my 7th great-grandmother. Ann was baptised 02 Apr 1676 in St. Peter, Thanet and on 21 April 1702 she married John Panterey (Pantry) in St. Lawrence in Thanet.

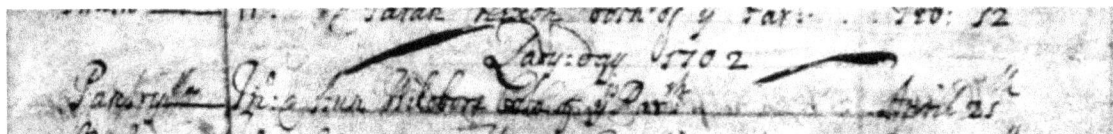

Marriage Record 1702

John was baptised 07 Jan 1671/72 in St. Lawrence as the son of John Panterey and Priscilla Curling. He died 20 Jan 1721/22.

8th Great-grandmother Priscilla Curling can be traced back to her baptism on 27 Apr 1638 in St. Lawrence, Thanet Kent to John Curling and Alice Powell. Alice was baptised 19 Sep 1613 and married John Curling 25 October 1632 in St. Lawrence.

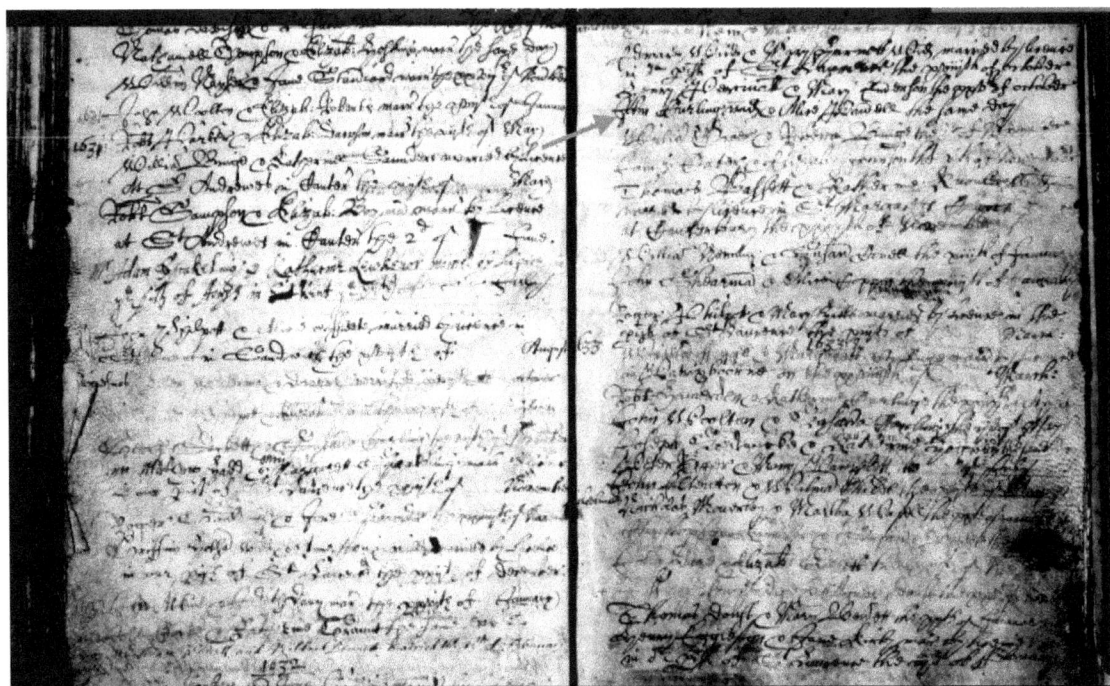

Marriage Record John Curling & Alice Powell

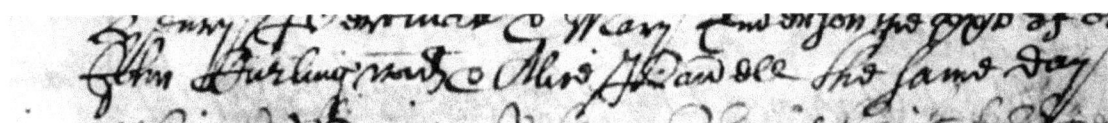

Cropped Marriage Record John Curling & Alice Powell

Notes

You may use this space to make your personal notes.

www.ingramcontent.com/pod-product-compliance
Lightning Source LLC
Chambersburg PA
CBHW051349290326
41933CB00042B/3349